CHRISTIAN HEROES:

# NATE SAINT

# Unit Study
## Curriculum Guide

# JANET & GEOFF BENGE

**PUBLISHING**
*A Ministry Of Youth With A Mission*
P.O. Box 55787, Seattle, WA 98155

YWAM Publishing is the publishing ministry of Youth With A Mission. Youth With A Mission (YWAM) is an international missionary organization of Christians from many denominations dedicated to presenting Jesus Christ to this generation. To this end, YWAM has focused its efforts in three main areas: (1) training and equipping believers for their part in fulfilling the Great Commission (Matthew 28:19), (2) personal evangelism (3) mercy ministry (medical and relief work).

For a free catalog of books and materials write or call
YWAM Publishing
P.O. Box 55787, Seattle, WA 98155
(425) 771-1153 or (800) 922-2143
www.ywampublishing.com

**Nate Saint: A Unit Study Curriculum Guide**
Copyright © 2000 by Janet and Geoff Benge

Published by Youth With A Mission Publishing
P.O. Box 55787
Seattle, WA 98155

ISBN 1-57658-187-X

Verses marked NIV are taken from the Holy Bible, New International Version®, Copyright © 1973, 1978, 1984 by the International Bible Society. Used by permission of Zondervan Publishing House.

**Printed in the United States of America**

# Contents

# NATE SAINT

## 1923–1956

# Nate Saint:
# A Unit Study Curriculum Guide

This unit study guide is designed to accompany the book *Nate Saint: On a Wing and a Prayer* from the Christian Heroes: Then & Now series by Janet and Geoff Benge. It provides the Christian schoolteacher and homeschooling parent with ways in which to use the book as a vehicle for teaching or reinforcing various curriculum areas, including

- creative writing
- drama
- movie critiquing
- reading comprehension
- essay writing
- history and geography concepts

As there are more ideas than could possibly be used in one unit, it is the parent/teacher's job to sift through the ideas and select those that best fit the needs of the students.

The activities recommended in this unit study guide are

- Reflective of a wide range of learning styles.
- Designed for both group and individual study.
- Suitable for a range of grade levels and abilities.

## Learning Styles

Choose those activities that are best suited to your student or students. For example, when studying the physical features of a country, a kinesthetic learner will learn best by producing a three-dimensional clay model representing the physical features of the country, whereas a visual learner will find it more meaningful to produce a poster map of the country for the classroom wall.

## Group or Individual Study

While the activities contained in this unit study guide are designed to be carried out by an individual student working alone, instructions are also provided for how to adapt an activity to a group situation.

## Grade Levels/Abilities

As you thumb through this unit study guide, you will note that grade levels are not assigned to particular activities, though some areas, essay topics for example, progress from the simple to the complex. This approach has been taken because students of varying grade levels can undertake most of the activities. For example, one of the activities suggests a student locate and interview a World War II veteran and then write a newspaper feature article based on his or her experiences. A fourth grader doing this activity would tend to comment on concrete objects, such as where the veteran served, how long he or she was away from home, and what his or her specific job was. By contrast, a ninth grader undertaking the same assignment would be able to explore more abstract concepts, such as how the veteran felt about going to war and about the response of the American public to returned servicemen, and how being a returned serviceman changed the rest of his or her life. Both students use the same activity and instructions to create work appropriate to their age and cognitive ability.

In the middle pages of this unit study guide you will find two foldout pages. These pages contain three maps and a fact sheet to be filled out by the student. The maps and fact sheet are designed to be photocopied onto individual pages so that each student can store them in his or her folder. They are for use with the social studies section of this unit study guide (chapter six).

Before you begin teaching from this unit study guide, please read through each section. You may wish to highlight the activities that appeal to you or that you know your students would enjoy or be challenged by. Many teachers find it useful to plan the culminating event (see chapter eight) first and then select a range of learning activities that lend themselves to this event.

For the sake of brevity in the instructions that accompany each section, the word *teacher* includes the homeschooling parent, and the word *student* refers to a child either in a traditional classroom or in a homeschool environment.

*1*

# Key Bible Verses

The authors have selected four relevant Bible verses that can be used alongside or as part of this unit study. For your convenience, these verses have been quoted in two versions: the King James Version and the New International Version. Of course, many other appropriate Bible verses can be added to the list if more are needed. The verses can be used in a number of ways, including the following:

*Memorization.* The teacher can assign one or all of the verses to be memorized during the duration of the study. A chart could be made to track which students have completed memorizing which verses.

*Meaning.* The verses can be used to spark conversations on the spiritual aspects of Nate's life. This can then be translated into action by having students form groups and present one of the verses to the class in a creative manner. Students could make up a skit to illustrate the meaning of the verse or present a one-act play to show how the verse was relevant in the life of Nate Saint.

*Devotional.* The teacher might also consider beginning a class or family devotional book. To do this, the teacher should familiarize the students with a variety of devotional writings and then ask them to write a devotion based upon their own understanding of one of the verses as it related to the life of Nate Saint. The pages could then be glued or copied into a blank book, illustrated, and signed. The various devotions could be read aloud at appropriate times, including during assemblies and family devotional times and at the culminating event.

*Display.* Students could also design a plaque, wall hanging, poster, or banner with one of the verses written on it. This could be hung in a prominent place while the unit study is being undertaken and used for decoration during the culminating event.

ᏬᎧᎧᎧᎧᎧᎧᎧᏇ

❝As every man hath received the gift, even so minister the same one to another, as good stewards of the manifold grace of God. If any man speak, let him speak as the oracles of God; if any man minister, let him do it as of the ability which God giveth: that God in all things may be glorified through Jesus Christ, to whom be praise and dominion for ever and ever. Amen.❞ (1 Peter 4:10-11 KJV)

❝Each one should use whatever gift he has received to serve others, faithfully administering God's grace in its various forms. If anyone speaks, he should do it as one speaking the very words of God. If anyone serves, he should do it with the strength God provides, so that in all things God may be praised through Jesus Christ. To him be the glory and the power for ever and ever. Amen.**99** (1 Peter 4:10-11 NIV)

☙❦❧

**66**And whatsoever ye do, do it heartily, as to the Lord, and not unto men; knowing that of the Lord ye shall receive the reward of the inheritance: for ye serve the Lord Christ.**99** (Colossians 3:23-24 KJV)

**66**Whatever you do, work at it with all your heart, as working for the Lord, not for men, since you know that you will receive an inheritance from the Lord as a reward. It is the Lord Christ you are serving.**99** (Colossians 3:23-24 NIV)

☙❦❧

**66**For whosoever will save his life shall lose it: but whosoever will lose his life for my sake, the same shall save it. For what is a man advantaged, if he gain the whole world, and lose himself, or be cast away?**99** (Luke 9:24-25 KJV)

**66**For whoever wants to save his life will lose it, but whoever loses his life for me will save it. What good is it for a man to gain the whole world, and yet lose or forfeit his very self?**99** (Luke 9:24-25 NIV)

☙❦❧

**66**Yea, though I walk through the valley of the shadow of death, I will fear no evil: for thou art with me; thy rod and thy staff they comfort me.**99** (Psalm 23:4 KJV)

66Even though I walk through the valley of the shadow of death, I will fear no evil, for you are with me; your rod and your staff, they comfort me.99 (Psalm 23:4 NIV)

# Display Corner

Many students will enjoy collecting and displaying objects from the country or culture they are studying. It is motivational to designate a corner of the room, including a table or desk and wall space, that can be used for this purpose. Keep some index cards on the table and encourage students to label their contributions, including as much information as possible about where their object came from, what it is used for, and who would use it.

Encourage students to ask their parents and friends if they have anything interesting (but not valuable) from Ecuador that they could bring to class. A visit to a South American grocery could also yield some very interesting display items, as would a trip to the local library to find books on Ecuador and famous Ecuadorans. Students might also like to bring photographs of their relatives who served in World War II or items about Missionary Aviation Fellowship. Below is a list of things students (or you) might like to display. Of course, there are many more options.

- A large map of Ecuador or the Amazon Basin.
- Products of Ecuador, especially Panama hats.
- Ecuadoran food, such as bananas, barley, cocoa, cassava, coffee, maize, potatoes, rice, sugarcane, and wheat, and related objects.
- Examples of Spanish writing, including Bibles and tracts. These are available through the American Bible Society at (212) 408-1200 or online at www.americanbible.org.
- Photographs and articles about Ecuador and the Amazon Basin, both in the past and in the present.
- Newspaper articles about Ecuador or the Amazon Basin that highlight current events in the various regions of the country.
- Ecuadoran stamps and coins.
- Dolls in native Ecuadoran dress.
- Photographs of relatives who served in World War II, along with a brief written description of where they served and what they did.
- Model planes made by the students.
- Articles or items having to do with Missionary Aviation Fellowship (see Appendix A for the MAF web site address where newsletters, posters, and photographs are available).

## 3

# Chapter Questions

There are four questions related to each chapter of *Nate Saint: On a Wing and a Prayer*:
1. A vocabulary question drawn from the text and referenced to a page in the book.
2. A factual question arising from the text.
3. A question to gauge the level of a student's comprehension.
4. An open-ended question seeking an opinion or interpretation.

These questions are designed for students to complete on their own. They are best answered after a student finishes reading each chapter in the book. Answers to the first three questions for each chapter are given in Appendix B of this guide. The answer to the fourth question is open-ended and needs to be evaluated separately. Since question four deals with a student's own interpretation or opinions, it is a good question on which to base a group discussion. Keep in mind that there is no right or wrong answer to question four, only positions a student needs to justify.

To gain maximum benefit from the questions, the students should write full-sentence answers and not just one or two words. For example, in response to the question, "How many brothers and sisters did Nate have?" they should write, "Nate Saint had five brothers and one sister," and not just "five and one."

Each vocabulary question asks the students to use the new word in a sentence. You have the option of having the students write a sentence using the new word. If you ask them to do this, make sure they write sentences that clearly demonstrate the meaning of the vocabulary word.

A supplement to answering the questions is to have students write a short summary of each chapter or write a response to the chapter in their journal. This could involve the students writing about how they relate to the character's actions, noting whether this is how they think they would react in a similar situation, and speculating as to what they think might happen next in the story.

## Chapter One

1. What is a biplane (page 15)? Use the word in a sentence.
2. How many brothers and sisters did Nate Saint have?
3. Why did the neighborhood children enjoy visiting the Saint house?
4. In many ways, Nate's parents were less strict than most parents. Why do you think this was?

## Chapter Two

1. What does diminish mean (page 27)? Use the word in a sentence.
2. What did Nate's brothers do to help Nate pass the time while he was sick in bed?
3. Why did Nate quit day school and begin night school instead?
4. Did Nate prefer to work with his hands or his head or both? Explain your answer.

## Chapter Three

1. What does transformation mean (page 45)? Use the word in a sentence.
2. What new hobby did Nate take up at the base in Amarillo, Texas?
3. Why did Nate want to learn more about CAMF?
4. What talents do you have that you think could be used to serve others in some way?

## Chapter Four

1. What does minimize mean (page 58)? Use the word in a sentence.
2. What was Nate wearing during his hike to Glacier Point?
3. What made Nate realize that he was following bear tracks and not human tracks?
4. Explain what Nate meant by an "unacceptable risk." Do you agree with him? Why or why not?

## Chapter Five

1. What are duplicates (page 63)? Use the word in a sentence.

2. How much did Nate's tools weigh?
3. Why did Nate need Santiago to help him put the Waco biplane back together?
4. Do you think it was a good idea for Nate to delay going to college and travel to Mexico to repair the plane? Why or why not?

## Chapter Six

1. What are blueprints (page 73)? Use the word in a sentence.
2. Why wouldn't the Waco's engine keep running?
3. What plane did Nate suggest MAF use in the future?
4. What character qualities do you think Marj would need to marry Nate and live in the jungle with him?

## Chapter Seven

1. What are prospectors (page 91)? Use the word in a sentence.
2. Who was already living at Shell Mera when Nate arrived?
3. Why did Nate start an English-speaking Sunday school in Shell Mera?
4. If you had to live in the Ecuadoran Oriente, what do you think you would find the most difficult?

## Chapter Eight

1. What does revert mean (page 103)? Use the word in a sentence.
2. What injuries did Nate receive in the plane accident?
3. Why did Nate argue that Christians are expendable?

4. Nate was prepared to risk his life as a missionary but not as a climber (refer to chapter four). Do you agree with his reasoning?

## Chapter Nine

1. What does ingenious mean (page 112)? Use the word in a sentence.
2. How many people lost their lives in airplane crashes within a hundred miles of Shell Mera in the six months after Nate had his accident?
3. What gave Nate inspiration for his emergency fuel bypass system?
4. Why do you think the Shell Oil Company sold its facility to MAF and the Berean Bible Institute for one tenth of its value?

## Chapter Ten

1. What does skewed mean (page 128)? Use the word in a sentence.
2. How many years were the Saints at Shell Mera before returning to the United States for a furlough?
3. Why was Rachel Saint so glad to hear about Dayuma?
4. Do you think Nate Saint would have been able to carry out his MAF work without Marj? Why or why not?

## Chapter Eleven

1. What does intrigued mean (page 136)? Use the word in a sentence.
2. What precautions did Nate take when transporting the aluminum sheets for the McCullys' roof?

3. Why did the Shell Oil Company pull out of Arajuno?
4. What qualities do you think missionaries like the McCullys needed to live in a place like Arajuno? Give reasons for your answer.

### Chapter Twelve

1. What is a machete (page 152)? Use the word in a sentence.
2. What was the first gift the missionaries dropped to the Aucas?
3. Why were the missionaries so cautious about meeting the Aucas?
4. What other gifts do you think would have been valuable or interesting to the Aucas? Why?

### Chapter Thirteen

1. What does apprehension mean (page 167)? Use the word in a sentence.
2. How much extra landing room was needed for every extra pound of weight in the plane?
3. Why did the missionaries agree not to shoot at the Auca warriors under any circumstances?
4. Do you think the missionaries could have done anything more to ensure their safety? Why or why not?

### Chapter Fifteen

1. What are coordinates (page 185)? Use the word in a sentence.
2. During the attack, who tried to contact Marj on the radio?
3. Why did the Waorani (Aucas) believe they had to kill the missionaries?

4. What do you think the Aucas thought about the missionaries? Why do you say that?

## Chapter Sixteen

1. What are gestures (page 196)? Use the word in a sentence.
2. For how many years did Nate's sister Rachel live with the Waorani?
3. Why were the Waorani suspicious when the missionary women went to live with them?
4. In what ways do you think the missionaries' actions helped the Waorani people to understand the idea of forgiveness? Explain your answer.

# Student Explorations

Student explorations are a variety of activities that are appropriate to a wide range of learning styles. These activities consist of the following:

*Essay Questions.* These are questions that can be used as essay writing ideas. Students can either be assigned a topic or choose their own from the list. The simplest essay topics appear first, followed in order by those that are more complex.

*Creative Writing.* This includes writing such things as newspaper articles, poems, letters, resumes, songs, and journals.

*Hands-On Projects.* These are various kinds of projects, such as charts and graphs, models, comic strips, family crests, mottoes, dioramas, book covers, and mobiles.

*Audio / Visual Projects.* These involve such things as using a tape recorder to conduct a mock interview or producing a radio play or commercial. A number of ways in which still and video cameras can be used to create dramatic presentations are discussed.

*Arts and Crafts.* These include art forms and crafts used in Ecuador.

*Language Examples.* Some examples of words written in Spanish are given. Students can use them to make banners or place mats for the culminating event or in their hands-on projects. For example, they could use a Spanish phrase as an alternative book title when creating a book cover.

*[Note on group projects: All the suggestions described below are individual learning activities. However, some of the activities have bracketed paragraphs like this one after them that offer suggestions on how the activity can be adapted for class or group use.]*

## Essay Questions

1. When Nate went to Ecuador in 1948, missionaries in remote areas lived outside of any daily contact with the outside world. Today through satellite links, digital phones, and e-mail, a missionary can be in instant contact with others. Write an essay describing the various ways in which you think these modern technologies have changed the role and lifestyle of the modern missionary.

2. Nate's parents adopted an unconventional style in child rearing. Describe that style and specific ways in which it may have helped Nate adjust to life in the Amazon jungle.

3. Research and write an essay describing the discovery and development of antibiotics and how they changed the shape of medicine. Trace how Nate's life may have been different had these drugs been available to him.

4. Nate was obviously surrounded by courageous women with strong convictions. Explore the roles of his mother, his wife Marj, and his sister Rachel, in the unfolding story of reaching the Waorani tribe.

5. Evaluate the following statement and give examples of why it might be true: "Nate Saint's innovations and technological know-how played a significant role in opening up the Amazon jungle to missionaries."

## Creative Writing

1. Read the summary of Nate's radio address on the topic of "expendability" (see pages 101-102). Write a poem that expresses your views on this subject.

2. Imagine you are Nate Saint. Write a letter to a friend explaining why you came to El Real to fix the airplane and describing some of the problems you have encountered. Keep in mind that Nate was a very lively writer.

3. Locate and interview a World War II veteran. Write a newspaper feature article based on his or her experiences.

4. Based on the information in the book, write a yearbook entry or a high school report card for Nate. Don't forget to include teacher comments.

5. The skeleton of Nate's Piper Cub is now on permanent display at MAF headquarters. Write a plaque that tells the story of how it got there.

**Hands-On Projects**

1.  Make a timeline of Nate Saint's life. On the time-line, record world events that occurred during Nate's lifetime.
    *[This can be an individual or a group effort.]*

2.  Recreate your version of the three postcards Nate sent from jail. Include text and a photograph on the front of each card.

3.  Select or make models of seven objects that represent various significant events in Nate Saint's life. Make a display explaining why you consider the objects to be significant. For example, you might include a piece of stained glass to represent Nate's father's occupation and a bucket on a rope to represent Nate's innovative bucket drop system.
    *[Coordinate the "artifacts" and present them in a display. Have students prepare an audio tour of the artifacts telling how they reflect various aspects of Nate Saint's life.]*

4.  Make a papier-mâché or clay topographical model of Ecuador and the Amazon jungle. Name the major rivers, mountain ranges, plains, seas, and oceans. Use flags to show Quito and Shell Mera.

5.  Draw an alternative book cover for the book. Give the book a new title, and be sure to write an exciting blurb for the back cover.

6.  Use cardboard cartons and other familiar objects to make a model of a Piper Cub. Label the various parts of the plane.

7.  Draw or paint a series of pictures that show the development of Shell Mera from the time it was

virgin jungle to the time of Nate's death. Label the changes to the landscape, along with when they occurred. (For example, in 1948, Nate built a taxiway to the hangar.)

8. Research the history of Ecuador and make a timeline that highlights major events, such as discovery by the Spanish and independence. Contrast this with the history of the United States.

9. Research the four ethnic groups that make up the Ecuadoran people. Make a pie chart showing the proportion of each and where they originated.

10. Create a brochure advertising an Amazon Adventure Excursion.

### Audio/Visual Projects

1. Recreate the way in which Nate demonstrated to Marj the principle of the bucket drop system (pages 108-109). Make a short documentary about this system and how Nate used it to communicate with people on the floor of the jungle.
   *[Alternatively, you could demonstrate the "flour bomb" method for measuring the length of a landing strip.]*

2. Create a version of *This Is Your Life* for Nate Saint. Choose key people who would have known him and set up a studio where "Nate" can meet them again. Videotape your production.

3. Write five monologues based on the lives of the five men who were martyred by the Waorani. Make sure that each monologue includes the person's background, how the person came to be involved in

Operation Auca, and why he believed it was important. Video a performance of these monologues. (You could break them up, doing each man's background first, then each man's reasons for being in Ecuador, followed by each man's reasons for being involved in the operation, and the like.)

4. The deaths of the missionaries were interpreted in different ways by different people. Role-play seven people who were affected differently by the deaths and have them tell why and how they were affected. Make an audio or videotape of the presentation.

### Arts and Crafts

1. The Amazon jungle is home to some of the world's most bizarre-looking wildlife. Research these animals and insects and make a papier-mâché model of one of them. Paint the model in the appropriate colors and label it for display.

2. The Waorani used clay pots and baskets for their food gathering and cooking. Make some clay pots (using a pinch or coil method) and fire them using a sawdust kiln. Or try making a basket from twigs and leaves.

3. The Waorani, like all other jungle people, were very familiar with the trees of the forest. Take bark rubbings and leaf prints from trees in your neighborhood. Compare and display them.

4. Nate loved to make models. Put together a model of an airplane or a train.

## Language Examples

Below are some examples of sentences written in Spanish. Use them to make banners, posters, and bookmarks, and use them on invitations or place mats for the culminating event.

*Jesus loves the little children.*
Jesús quiere a los niños.

✺

*God is Love.*
Dios es amor.

✺

*Pray for the people of Ecuador.*
Rece por la gente del Ecuador.

✺

*Jesus said, "I am the light of the world."*
Jesús dijo—Soy la luz del mundo.

# Community Links

Many communities have a rich supply of people and places to which students can be exposed to help them learn about and appreciate other cultures. It is well worth the effort to find out what your community has to offer with regard to the unit you are studying. For this unit, for example, you may be able to host a missionary who has worked in Ecuador or visit a nearby airfield.

While it would be wonderful if you could take a field trip to visit some of these people and places, if you can't, it is often possible to have visitors come to the classroom. Whether you decide to take a field trip or invite a guest to your classroom, such activities need to be flanked by sound educational choices. Otherwise much of the educational value of the event will not be realized. The following three steps will help students derive the greatest educational value from a field trip or classroom visit.

## Step One: Preparation

Students should always research the topic before they begin a classroom interview or field trip. In doing so, they will be ready to ask intelligent questions based upon a sound knowledge of their topic. For example, if a class is going to visit an airfield, the students need to know something about aviation during the 1950s (when the book takes place) so that they can find out what has changed since then. With this in mind, they can ask such questions as: Do modern planes have some way to get fuel to the engine if the fuel line is blocked? Are seat belts compulsory in airplanes? What is the most dangerous terrain to fly over now? Why?

As the teacher, you need to give the students a clear idea as to why they are going on the field trip and what they are expected to produce with their findings. For example, you might say to them, "We are going to visit an airfield and talk to a pilot. When we get back, you are going to be making a Venn diagram of the similarities and differences between small planes today and small planes like those Nate Saint flew during the 1950s."

Students should be encouraged to compile lists of questions they want answers to, based upon what they have already learned. They should carry a clipboard with them to write down answers, draw sketches, and note observations. (For less motivated students, a simple worksheet of activities to be completed on the field trip itself can be a good idea.) Such activities reinforce the idea that the field trip is a serious educational event and that the student is there to gather information, not just to be a sightseer.

### Step Two: The Event

During the actual field trip or classroom visit, make sure that the students remain on task. Insist that they be respectful of property and other people at all times. Designate a spokesperson to thank whomever you talk to as well as the parents who help with the event.

### Step Three: Processing and Reflection

Students should be given time to process the information they have gathered from their field trip or classroom visit and reflect on it, both individually and as a class. This can take many forms, including making flowcharts or diagrams of what they learned, editing interviews for articles or audiovisual presentations, writing reports, and making booklets. Something as simple as a class book called *Did You Know?* in which each student writes down one fact he or she learned from the field trip, can serve as an effective reflection tool.

### Suggested Community Links

*Amazon Missionaries.* Ask around to see if you can find a missionary who has worked in the Amazon Basin. If so, invite the person to speak to your class. Ask the person to bring along any artifacts he or she has. This will make the visit more memorable for the students.

*Ecuadoran People.* Find a person from Ecuador who can tell you about his or her country and family's history. How long has the family been in the United States? What part of Ecuador is the family from?

Which language(s) does the family speak? Can the person write or speak something in that language for your class? What does the person like to eat at home? What Ecuadoran customs does the family still practice in America?

*Aviation Related.* Invite a pilot or an aircraft mechanic to speak to your class about his or her work or, alternatively, visit a nearby airfield or airport to learn about aviation today.

*Veterans.* Invite a World War II veteran to tell the class about his or her experiences. Compare and contrast these to Nate's experiences.

*Missionary Aviation Fellowship.* Locate someone who has worked with MAF and invite the person to speak to the class about his or her experiences.

*Travel Agent.* Locate a travel agent who specializes in tours to South America. Invite him or her to speak to the class about how to get to Ecuador and what preparations to make, along with some of the interesting things visitors like to see while there.

# 6

# Social Studies

The social studies section is divided into five categories, each with suggestions on how to use the material given. The categories are briefly described below.

*Places/Locations.* This section covers places named in the text of the book *Nate Saint: On a Wing and a Prayer.*

*Journeys.* This category covers journeys undertaken by Nate Saint.

*Terms/Vocabulary.* This section gives ideas for studying some of the terms used in the book.

*Geographical Characteristics.* This section contains questions about the physical characteristics of Ecuador.

*Conceptual Questions.* This section provides the teacher with conceptual social studies questions related to the book.

Ecuador

N →

United
States

N

The World

N

# ECUADOR FACT SHEET

**South America**

**Ecuador**

**Official Name of Country:** _____

**Type of Government:** _____

**Current Head of State:** _____

**Capital City:** _____

**Size of Country:** _____

**Population:** _____

**Main Religions:**

| | Name | Percentage of Population |
|---|---|---|
| 1 | | |
| 2 | | |
| 3 | | |
| 4 | | |

**Literacy Rate:** _____

**Main Exports:** _____

## Places/Locations

These places are categorized by country, with the page number where they are first referred to in the book given in parentheses. Students can undertake a range of activities with these place names. They can

- Locate and mark the places on the relevant country map. (Maps for this purpose are located in the foldout map section in the center of this guide.)
- Note other points, such as their absolute location (latitude and longitude), and then observe how this location compares to other locations mentioned in the book. For example, calculate which location is closer to the equator or the North Pole.
- Calculate the relative locations of various places mentioned in the book. For example, how far is it from Huntingdon to El Real, Mexico, or from Quito to Shell Mera?
- Construct a key to show the population density in the Amazon Basin or Ecuador.
- Pinpoint the places on a large wall map in the classroom. Students can then use index cards to write explanations as to why the various places are mentioned in the story. Each card could be pinned to the wall with a length of yarn connecting it to the appropriate place on the map.

*Places mentioned in the United States*

Huntingdon (page 16)
Philadelphia (page 16)
Pennsylvania (page 16)
Delaware River (page 16)

Washington D.C. (page 17)
Abington (page 21)
New Jersey (page 22)
Poconoes (page 26)

Virginia (page 30)
Bluefield, Virginia (page 31)
New York City (page 32)
Las Vegas, New Mexico (page 34)
Sangre Mountains (page 34)
Los Angeles (page 35)
Mojave Desert (page 35)
St. Louis, Missouri (page 35)
Sioux City, Iowa (page 36)
Amarillo, Texas (page 42)
Fort Wayne, Indiana (page 44)
Winona Lake, Indiana (page 44)
Detroit (page 45)

Salinas, California (page 50)
Merced, California (page 50)
Yosemite National Park (page 51)
Glacier Point (page 51)
Missouri River (page 63)
Kansas (page 63)
Laredo, Texas (page 63)
Texas/Mexico border (page 63)
Nevada (page 85)
Glendale, California (page 123)
Redlands, California (page 199)
Florida (page 200)

## Places mentioned in Ecuador

Mt. Sangay (page 83)
Amazon Basin (page 83)
Quito (page 84)
Andes Mountains (page 84)
Oriente (page 85)
Mera (page 86)
Shell Mera (page 86)
Macuma (page 88)
Dos Rios (page 89)
Napo River (page 91)

Villano River (page 91)
Arajuno River (page 91)
Peruvian border (page 91)
Arapicos (page 110)
Ambato (page 113)
Curaray River (page 133)
Shandia (page 140)
Puyupunga (page 140)
Villano (page 145)
"Palm Beach" (page 161)

## Other locations mentioned

Japan (page 32)
Pearl Harbor, Hawaii (page 32)
Sicily (page 39)
Pacific Ocean (page 40)
South America (page 49)
Mexico (page 49)
Peru (page 49)
El Real, Mexico (page 62)
Mexico Ciy (page 64)

Guatemala (page 65)
Chiapas, Mexico (page 65)
Tuxtla Gutierrez (page 65)
Pijijiapan, Mexico (page 65)
Venustiano, Mexico (page 65)
Huimanguillo, Mexico (page 65)
Ecuador (page 83)
Atlantic Ocean (page 83)
Panama (page 98)

## Journeys

Using the journeys listed below, students can
- Map the journeys on the relevant map.
- Add details to the map from the story, such as how long each leg of the journey took, when the person started and finished the journey, and the kinds of transportation the person used along the way.
- Compare the journeys Nate took to taking the same journeys today. Students could research how they might reach those destinations today, how long it would take to get there, and how much it would cost.

*Major journeys Nate took*

1. Nate's postings during World War II.
2. Nate's journey from Huntingdon to El Real, Mexico.

## Terms/Vocabulary

Below is a list of terms used in the book. The page number where the term is first used is given in parentheses. The list covers a range of terms from the simple to the advanced. Students can use this list to
- Define and memorize the terms. You may find it helpful to asterisk or highlight in some way those terms you think would be appropriate for your particular students. If they know the meaning of all but five of the terms, have them learn only those five. Conversely, if they are unfamiliar with most of the terms, choose a realistic number for each student to explore and learn.

- Produce an individual or class reference book of terms. Assign each student a set number of terms to write a definition for or draw a sketch of. From this research, a book of definitions can be made, with one page allotted for each definition. This book could be added to throughout the year. (Students may need a dictionary to help them here.)
- Play reinforcement games such as *Go Fish.* To do this, draw some of the sketched definitions from the list compiled in the point above onto index cards and  have the students take turns pairing them with written definitions.

### *Terms/vocabulary*

province (page 65)
adobe brick (page 68)
jungle (page 71)
peak (page 83)
active volcano (page 83)
lava (page 83)
coastal lowlands (page 85)
export (page 85)
rain forest (page 85)
acre (page 87)
cultivate (page 92)
elevation (page 99)
equator (page 101)
atmospheric interference
    (page 101)

earth's magnetic field (page 101)
frontier (page 124)
Stone Age (page 131)
plantation (page 133)
reclaimed (page 135)
territory (page 142)
village (page 143)
settlements (page 145)
valleys (page 146)
crosswind (page 147)
culture (page 148)
sandbar (page 154)
upstream (page 155)
site (page 157)

## Geographical Characteristics

Have students use an atlas to locate the following and then mark them on the blank map of Ecuador from the foldout map section in the center of this book:

- Ecuador's seven major rivers, their sources, and courses: the Aguarico, Curaray, Esmeraldas, Guayas, Napo, Pastaza, and Zamora.
- The three main regions of Ecuador.
- Ecuador's volcanoes.
- The seven largest cities in Ecuador.
- The Andes Mountains.
- The latitude and longitude lines that bisect Ecuador.
- The Pacific Ocean and the Gulf of Guayaquil.
- The countries Ecuador shares borders with: Colombia and Peru.
- The Galapagos Islands.

## Conceptual Questions

The following questions are ordered from the simple to the complex. You could ask the students to use these questions to

- Write one or more paragraphs to answer each question.
- Present an oral report to the class on one of the questions.
- Discuss the answer(s) to a question or questions in a group context.

*Questions to ponder (simple to complex)*

1. Locate and name two countries that are larger than Ecuador, two countries that are about the same size, and two countries that are a lot smaller.
2. Using a map, arrange the countries of South America in order from the largest to the smallest. Where does Ecuador fit in this list?

3. How large is Ecuador compared to the United States?

4. What is the population of Ecuador compared to the population of the United States?

5. Two countries share borders with Ecuador. Using encyclopedias, newspapers, or other community resources, try to work out whether these countries have strained or friendly relations with Ecuador.

6. Study a physical map of Ecuador. Where do you think most of the population would live? Why? Use a population map to test your hypothesis. Were you right or wrong? Why?

7. Find a map that shows the known oil deposits in the Amazon Basin. How much oil is estimated to be under the Amazon Basin? How does this compare with oil deposits in other parts of the world?

# 7

# Related Themes to Explore

Any unit study has natural links to many other topics that can also be explored. While it is impossible to pursue all such links in this context, the spoke diagram on the next page shows some related topics that students might find interesting to study alongside Nate Saint.

There are two ways you might like to integrate some of these links into your classroom. Some teachers and parents have the flexibility to be able to choose the topics their students study and even to alter their selections partway through the year. If you are able to do this, use the theme wheel to help identify other topics you might like to follow up this unit with. For example, after studying Nate Saint, your class might become interested in the developing role of airplanes in World War II or the role of Missionary Aviation Fellowship in world missions today.

Other teachers and parents are locked in to a less flexible curriculum. If this is your situation, you may still have the ability to change the order in which various topics are taught. Look through the topics listed to see whether any coincide with topics you have already scheduled for later in the year. Consider the possibility of scheduling the teaching of these topics closer to this unit so that cross-curriculum learning can take place.

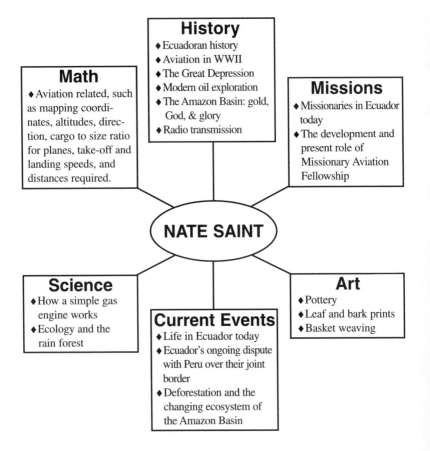

**History**
- Ecuadoran history
- Aviation in WWII
- The Great Depression
- Modern oil exploration
- The Amazon Basin: gold, God, & glory
- Radio transmission

**Math**
- Aviation related, such as mapping coordinates, altitudes, direction, cargo to size ratio for planes, take-off and landing speeds, and distances required.

**Missions**
- Missionaries in Ecuador today
- The development and present role of Missionary Aviation Fellowship

**NATE SAINT**

**Science**
- How a simple gas engine works
- Ecology and the rain forest

**Current Events**
- Life in Ecuador today
- Ecuador's ongoing dispute with Peru over their joint border
- Deforestation and the changing ecosystem of the Amazon Basin

**Art**
- Pottery
- Leaf and bark prints
- Basket weaving

## 8

# Culminating Event

As adults, we like to have a reason to learn something. We learn a new computer program so that we can balance our checking account, a song so that we can sing it at a wedding, or the rudiments of another language so that we are able to find our way around in a foreign country. Students have the same need for purpose in their learning. It is valid but not very motivational to tell a student he or she needs to gather and learn information to pass a test or move up a grade. It is much more motivational for a student when he or she has some other, more meaningful goal in mind. This goal can be a specific forum through which each student can express his or her newly acquired knowledge. We believe that part of the role of the teacher is to provide such a forum, which we call the culminating event.

As the name implies, the culminating event marks the end of the unit study and gives a sense of closure to the topic. It also serves to put what students have learned into a larger context that can then be shared with others.

The culminating event can be as simple as inviting the class next door (or the homeschooled children down the street) to come and hear poems and stories and view the written work that students have completed. Conversely, it could be as involved as hosting a parent/neighborhood dinner featuring Ecuadoran food and presentations on the life and achievements of Nate Saint.

No matter how simple or elaborate the culminating event is, make sure you have the broad outline of it in mind before planning the other activities for your unit study, as the two are integrally linked.

### Idea Sparks

*Food.* Prepare and serve regional food. The people of Ecuador love getting together for a meal, and nearly all of their religious holidays involve feasting. Tables tend to be a little higher, more chest height, and it is normal to eat with both elbows propped up on the table. A knife, held in the right hand, is used for cutting, and the fork, held in the left hand, is used curved side up to get the food into the mouth. Ecuadorans do not put their knife down and change hands. At the end of the meal, bread is often used to soak up any extra liquid on the plate.

A wide variety of fruits and vegetables are eaten in Ecuador. They include oranges, coconuts, lemons, bananas, avocados, pineapple, eggplant, and onions. Some favorite dishes are locro soup, made with avocados, cheese, and potato; secode pollo, stewed chicken with rice and avocado slices; empanadas, hot, crispy meat- or cheese-filled pastries; lomo salteado, beefsteak covered with onions and tomatoes; seco de chivo, goat stew (lamb could be substituted) served with rice; tortillas de maiz, corn tortillas; and ceviche, a variety of seafood marinated in lemon with onions and served with popcorn. Most dishes are accompanied by *ajji*, a hot sauce used for dipping.

Fruit juices are very popular, including orange, blackberry, guanaboan, passion fruit, manacuya, and papaya. Coffee is also consumed in large quantities. You will be able to find many of these items in an Hispanic grocery store.

*Music.* Play traditional Ecuadoran music in the background to set the mood. (Many libraries stock ethnic music selections. The Ecuadorans are well known for their flute playing.)

*Oral Presentations.* Present poems, essays, speeches, reports, reviews, and devotions that students have written during the course of the unit study.

*Display.* Display other work, including artwork, map work, models, newspapers, and video interviews.

*Clothing.* Younger students might enjoy dressing up, girls in long skirts and embroidered blouses and boys in ponchos. Both men and women wear felt hats.

*Cultural Activities.* Play traditional South American children's games.

# —— *Appendix A* ——

# Books and Resources

This appendix is divided into six sections: (1) another biography of Nate Saint, (2) related books, (3) related movies and documentaries, (4) other related books in the Christian Heroes: Then & Now series, (5) related articles from *National Geographic,* (6) Internet sites.

Some of the books listed here are more difficult to get copies of than others. If they are not available at your local Christian bookstore, many of the titles can be located in secondhand bookstores (try using the Internet to locate them). Most of the titles are also available through the national interlibrary loan service.

### Another Biography of Nate Saint

The biography listed on the bibliography page of *Nate Saint: On a Wing and a Prayer* is listed here. The listing has basic information on how to locate the book, including its ISBN number. The approximate age level of the intended reader is also given, along with the number of pages in the book and some comments to help you decide whether you might want to include the book in your unit study. Many of the books about Nate Saint are written at a higher reading level than the books in the Christian Heroes: Then & Now series and would be interesting for a teacher to read for his or her own information and as background for the unit. Children learn best by example, so consider choosing one good adult biography to read and enrich your own understanding of the topic.

TITLE:      *Jungle Pilot*
Author:     Russell T. Hitt
Publisher:  Discovery House Publishers, 1997
ISBN:       1572930225
Age Level:  Adult

Synopsis: This book covers in detail each phase of Nate Saint's life. Nate's wife Marj collaborated on the project, which includes many quotes from Nate's own journals and letters. At the end of the book, Nate's son Steve updates the story, including what has happened among the Waorani (Aucas) since the deaths of the five men.

Comments: This book is well worth purchasing. It is fairly easy to read. It has 302 pages, including 33 black-and-white photographs.

### Related Books

This section contains a list of books that fit around the life story of Nate Saint. ISBN numbers, age level, and relevant comments are included for each book listed.

Of course, there are many other books that relate in some way to this topic. You may want to record inside the back cover of this unit study guide the titles of other books you find particularly helpful.

TITLE:       *Through Gates of Splendor*
Author:      Elisabeth Elliot
Publisher:   Tyndale House, 1981
ISBN:        0842371524
Age Level:   Adult

Synopsis: Jim Elliot's wife Elisabeth (Betty) wrote this book on behalf of the five widows. It is a thorough account of the lives of the five men and the events that preceded and followed their martyrdom.

Comments: Several chapters are largely the reconstruction of Nate Saint's diary entries or letters. The book is 272 pages, including 75 photographs and a good map of the area.

TITLE:       *Shadow of the Almighty*
Author:      Elisabeth Elliot
Publisher:   HarperCollins, 1958 (updated 1989)
ISBN:        006062213
Age Level:   Adult

Synopsis: This is the story of Jim Elliot, the leader of the fated expedition, as told by his wife. Approximately the last third of the book deals with Ecuador and the events leading up to the men's deaths.

Comments: This is a good book to use to gain more understanding about Operation Auca and its ramifications. Large sections are quotes from Jim Elliot's journals and letters. This is a very well written and readable book. It has an excellent Scripture indexing system. It runs 250 pages, including 26 photographs.

TITLE: *Dayuma: Life Under Waorani Spears*
Author: Ethel Emily Wallis
Publisher: YWAM Publishing, 1996
ISBN: 0927545918
Age Level: Adult

Synopsis: These 204 pages tell the story of Dayuma, the young woman who fled her tribe to work on a plantation. Dayuma became the first contact Jim Elliot had with the Waorani and was able to provide enough language information for the team to proceed with Operation Auca. Dayuma went on to become the first Waorani Christian.

Comments: Dayuma's story intersects those of Nate Saint, Jim and Betty Elliot, and Rachel Saint at many points. It is powerfully written and fills in many of the details about what happened to the tribe after the missionaries' deaths.

TITLE: *The Fate of the Yellow Woodbee*
Author: Dave and Neta Jackson
Publisher: Bethany House, 1992
ISBN: 1556612451
Age Level: 8-12 years

Synopsis: This is a fictionalized account of a Waorani boy who becomes involved with Nate Saint and his airplane.

Comments: Although Niwa is a fictional character, many of the events in the story did happen. The story gives some context to Nate and MAF's work in the area.

## Related Movies and Documentaries

Listed in this section are movies and documentaries that have been made about the life of Nate Saint or issues and/or people who have some relationship to events in his life. The rating for each movie or documentary is included, but as with all unfamiliar material, it is prudent to preview them before showing them to the class.

Movies and documentaries are particularly useful in showing the visual details of another place and time period. As students watch, encourage them to study the clothing, weather, crops, terrain, and other geographical factors shown in the movie or documentary.

TITLE:     *The Great Air Race of 1924*
Type:      PBS documentary
Length:    60 minutes

Comments: This documentary follows four aviators and their mechanics on the first attempt at circling the globe in an airplane. The race takes place in 1924 and showcases the first attempts at proving that flying was a safe, reliable means of transport. The documentary uses over 500 still photographs along with entries from logs, diaries, eyewitness accounts, and contemporary movie footage to tell this fascinating story. It should definitely be viewed by anyone interested in the history of flight. It shows clearly the risks early pilots took. This adventure takes place in 1924, the year after Nate Saint was born, and the race would be interesting to contrast with the advances in aviation as Nate grew up. An interested student could make a timeline of aviation breakthroughs and plot them beside events in Nate's life, uncluding Nate's aviation exploits.

TITLE:     *Land of the Flooded Forest*
Type:      National Geographic documentary, 1990
Length:    50 minutes

Comments: This is an excellent documentary about the interplay of land and water in the Amazon Basin.

TITLE:      *Ecuador and the Galapagos Islands*
Type:      documentary, 1997
Length:    47 minutes

Comments: The documentary first takes the viewer on a trip by train from the coast up to Quito, the capital city. The film then explores the northern Amazon jungle, where the host and narrator spends time with a tribal group. Lastly, it shows a yacht trip to the Galapagos Islands. This documentary gives a great general overview of Ecuador. It shows the national dish, fried guinea pig, being prepared and eaten and an initiation rite in which a hallucinogenic liquid is consumed. You may want to preview these two scenes ahead of time.

TITLE:      *Creatures of the Amazon: Best of Bill Burrud Collection*
Type:      documentary, 1996
Length:    NA

Comments: An adventurer's look at the animals of the Amazon and their ecosystem.

TITLE:      *Warriors of the Amazon*
Type:      documentary, 1996
Length:    NA

Comments: This story of another Amazon tribe, the Yanomami, gives an accurate picture of their way of life, including their use of hallucinogenic drugs, magic practices, and consumption of human body ashes and their naked "dress." This would give the mature student a real understanding of the challenges that confront missionaries to the Amazon tribes. However, be sure to preview this and gain parental permission before showing it.

TITLE:        *Journey of a Thousand Rivers: Cousteau*
              *Collection, Vol. 7*
Type:         documentary
Length:       NA

Comments: A great documentary following the tributaries that lead into the Amazon River.

## Related Christian Heroes: Then & Now Books

TITLE:        *Jim Elliot: One Great Purpose*
Authors:      Janet and Geoff Benge
Publisher:    YWAM Publishing, 1999
ISBN:         1576581462

Comments: This is the story of the man who led Operation Auca. Jim Elliot (1927-1956) was four years younger than Nate Saint, but they shared the same desire to reach the inhabitants of the Amazon jungle with the gospel.

TITLE:        *Betty Greene: Wings to Serve*
Authors:      Janet and Geoff Benge
Publisher:    YWAM Publishing, 1999
ISBN:         1576581527

Comments: Betty Greene (1920-1997) served as a pilot in World War II and then went on to co-found Missionary Aviation Fellowship with Jim Truxton. Nate corresponded with Betty about joining MAF, and the two came to know each other well.

## Related National Geographic Articles

Many magazines have articles related to this topic. We have chosen to reference *National Geographic* because it can provide contemporaneous commentary on many events, since it dates back to the 1880s, and because it is widely available in libraries and schools throughout the country.

These articles and their accompanying photographs represent just some of those available that bear on aspects of Nate Saint's life. They can be used in a variety of ways to support and reinforce this unit study. For example, you could have students read the article "Mrs. Robinson Crusoe in Ecuador" (February 1934) and compare and contrast the difficulties Nate and Marj Saint encountered when setting up a home in the jungle with those the author encountered. A student could also be asked to make a chart of the similarities and differences between the Waorani and the Jivaro tribes, using the article "Over Trail and Through Jungle in Ecuador" (October 1921) to give an idea of what the Jivaros were like before they had contact with Europeans. Alternatively, students may find it interesting to design a poster aimed at recruiting Army Air Corps mechanics during World War II. They could glean some interesting statistics from the article "They Sustain the Wings" (September 1943) to help them.

*Articles about Ecuador and the Amazon Basin*

These articles were written during Nate Saint's lifetime (1923-1956).

TITLE:        The Volcanoes of Ecuador: Guideposts in
              Crossing South America.
Issue Date:   January 1929, pages 49-93

Description: An interesting article, particularly as it shows what was known about Ecuador during Nate's youth.

TITLE:       A Journey by the Jungle Rivers to the Home
             of the Cock-of-the-Rock
Issue Date:  November 1933, pages 585-630

Description:  A National Geographic team journeys into
the Amazon Basin to catalog previously unknown birds and
animals. This article contains many great photographs.

TITLE:       From Sea to Clouds in Ecuador
Issue Date:  December 1941, pages 717-740

Description:  A general introduction to Ecuador, including
its main trading items. Wonderful photographs are
included, depicting work at the Port of Guayaquil and
Quito.

TITLE:       Quinine Hunters in Ecuador
Issue Date:  March 1946, pages 341-363

Description:  Westerners come to the Amazon jungle looking for quinine. An excellent contemporary look at jungle
conditions and equipment used in the jungle.

TITLE:       Mrs. Robinson Crusoe in Ecuador
Issue Date:  February 1934, pages 133-172

Description:  This is a fascinating account, with many
great photographs, written by the wife of an American eth-
nologist. The author writes about the challenges of setting
up a home in the jungle.

TITLE:       El Sangay, Fire-Breathing Giant of the Andes
Issue Date:  January 1950, pages 117-138

Description:  A fascinating article about El Sangay, the
volcano that Nate could see so clearly from his living room.
Wonderful photographs of the people who live around the
volcano complement this article.

TITLE:        Jungle Jaunt on Amazon Headwaters
Issue Date:   September 1952, pages 371-388

Description: The story of a white woman and her Indian guides as they travel through the remote jungles of Colombia and Brazil. The script is lively and tells of the reactions of natives who have never seen a white woman before.

*Articles of interest about Ecuador*

TITLE:        Over Trail and Through Jungle in Ecuador
Issue Date:   October 1921, pages 327-352

Description:  A graphic look at the culture of the head-hunting Jivaros Indians, including photographs of shrunken heads. (Nate's friend, Frank Drown, worked among the Jivaros. See page 140 of *Nate Saint: On a Wing and a Prayer.*)

TITLE:        Brazil's Wild Frontier
Issue Date:   November 1977, pages 684-719

Description: This author explores the inner tributaries of the Amazon River by airplane, jeep, and riverboat and on foot. Good insights are given into the challenges of travel in the Amazon Basin.

TITLE:        Ecuador—Low and Lofty Land Astride the
              Equator
Issue Date:   December 1968, pages 259-298

Description: This article gives an overview of Ecuador, including the Andes, Amazon jungle, coastal deserts, and stunning photographs of Quito.

*Articles about aviation*

TITLE:       They Sustain the Wings
Issue Date:  September 1943, pages 333-354

Description: This article describes the role of mechanics and other nonflying staff in keeping the U.S. Air Force airborne during World War II. It is filled with details about the training and life Nate Saint would have had in the Army Air Corps. This article is a great resource.

TITLE:       Our Air Age Speeds Ahead
Issue Date:  February 1948, page 249-272

Description: An excellent source of information and photographs outlining the "latest" in airplane technology.

TITLE:       Aviation Looks Ahead on Its 50th Birthday;
             50 Years of Flight
Issue Date:  December 1953, pages 721-739; 740-756

Description: These two articles in the same edition provide a wonderful introduction to the history of aviation through its first fifty years.

## Internet Web Sites

### www.maf.org

This is the official web site of Missionary Aviation Fellowship. The site provides information on the work of MAF today. It has sections on news from around the world as well as highlights from MAF newsletters and prayer links. You can also buy posters, videos, books, and a VBS curriculum and subscribe to a free newsletter.

www.i-tecusa.org

This is the site of the Indigenous People's Technology and Education Center, an organization run by Steve Saint, Nate's son. The organization finds ways to partner with Waorani Christians to help meet the needs of the tribe. The site includes Amazon tours, maps, up-to-date photographs, ongoing projects, and general news of the tribe.

In addition to accessing these two specific sites, if you go to your search engine and type in "Ecuador" or "Amazon jungle" you will find a large number of sites that yield general information on weather, population, tourist packages, currency, government, and the like.

# *Appendix B*

# Answers to Chapter Questions

### Chapter One

1. A biplane is airplane with two sets of wings, one above the other.
2. Nate had five brothers and one sister.
3. The neighborhood children enjoyed visiting the Saints' house because there were always so many different things for them to do.

### Chapter Two

1. Diminish means to make smaller.
2. Nate's brothers visited him and told him stories about their activities.
3. Nate quit day school because he became restless when he sat around for too long.

### Chapter Three

1. Transformation means a complete change of appearance or character.

2. Nate took up photography while he was at the base in Amarillo.
3. Nate wanted to learn more about CAMF because he saw it as a possible way that he could fly and be a missionary at the same time.

## Chapter Four

1. Minimize means to reduce to the smallest degree.
2. Nate was wearing coveralls and two sweaters during his hike.
3. Nate noticed that the tracks were wide and that they were not boot prints.

## Chapter Five

1. Duplicates are copies.
2. Nate's tools weighed forty pounds.
3. Nate needed Santiago to help him because he was not skilled enough at woodworking to make all of the wooden parts.

## Chapter Six

1. Blueprints are building plans.
2. The Waco's engine wouldn't keep running because there were mud wasps in the fuel tank.
3. Nate suggested that MAF use lighter weight airplanes.

## Chapter Seven

1. Prospectors are people who explore a region looking for natural resources.
2. Workers from the Shell Oil Company were already in Shell Mera.

3. Nate started an English-speaking Sunday school because two little girls from the base had asked him when Sunday school would be starting.

### Chapter Eight

1. Revert means to go back to.
2. Nate had a compression fracture in his back and a pulled ligament in his left ankle.
3. Nate argued that Christians are expendable because they belong to God and, since they are going to spend eternity with Him, they need to let themselves be used up by God.

### Chapter Nine

1. Ingenious means being good at finding solutions to problems and at discovering or inventing something.
2. Fifty-one people lost their lives in airplane crashes within a hundred miles of Shell Mera during the six months after Nate had his accident.
3. A boy sitting on the roof of a truck with a five-gallon can of gas and a siphon tube inspired Nate to develop his emergency fuel bypass system.

### Chapter Ten

1. Skewed means twisted or slanted.
2. The Saints lived in Shell Mera for three years before they took their first furlough.
3. Rachel Saint was glad to hear about Dayuma because it gave her a way to study the Auca language without putting herself in danger.

## Chapter Eleven

1. Intrigued means to be fascinated by or interested in something.
2. Nate would not allow anyone in the airplane with him when he was flying with aluminum sheets in the sling under the plane.
3. The Shell Oil Company pulled out of Arajuno because it could not get Indian workers to work there after the Auca attacks.

## Chapter Twelve

1. A machete is a wide, heavy knife often used for cutting crops or long grass.
2. The first gift the missionaries dropped to the Aucas was a small kettle with buttons and salt in it.
3. The missionaries were cautious about meeting the Aucas because they knew that the Auca society was based on revenge and that white people had done some bad things to the Aucas in the past.

## Chapter Thirteen

1. Apprehension means fear or anxiety about something that might occur in the future.
2. An additional foot of landing room was needed for every extra pound of weight in the airplane.
3. The missionaries agreed not to shoot at the Auca warriors because they did not want to kill someone while trying to tell them about a loving, peaceful God.

## Chapter Fifteen

1. Coordinates are the two letters or numbers used to

fix a position on a map or graph.
2. Roger Youdarian tried to contact Marj on the radio during the attack.
3. The Waorani believed they had to kill the missionaries because if they didn't, the missionaries would kill them.

## Chapter Sixteen

1. Gestures are movements of the hand or body that convey meaning.
2. Rachel Saint lived with the Waorani for thirty-eight years.
3. The Waorani were suspicious because they thought the women might be spying on them and planning revenge.